NICHOLAS WRIGHT

Nicholas Wright's plays include *Vincent in Brixton* (Olivier Award for Best New Play, 2003) and the original production of *Mrs Klein*, at the National Theatre, in the West End and in New York; *Rattigan's Nijinsky* at Chichester Festival Theatre; *Treetops* and *One Fine Day* at Riverside Studios; *The Gorky Brigade* at the Royal Court; *The Crimes of Vautrin* for Joint Stock; *The Custom of the Country* and *The Desert Air* for the RSC; *Cressida* for the Almeida and *The Reporter* at the National. Adaptations include *His Dark Materials*, *Three Sisters* and *John Gabriel Borkman* for the National; *Thérèse Raquin* at Chichester Festival Theatre and the National; and *Naked* and *Lulu* at the Almeida, where *Mrs Klein* was also revived in 2009. He wrote the ballet scenario for Christopher Wheeldon's *Alice's Adventures in Wonderland* for the Royal Ballet, the libretti for Rachel Portman's opera *The Little Prince* (Houston Grand Opera) and for Jonathan Dove's opera for television, *Man on the Moon*, based on the Apollo 11 Moon landing. Other writing for television includes adaptations of *More Tales of the City* and *The No. 1 Ladies' Detective Agency* (BBC/HBO). His writing about the theatre includes *99 Plays*, a personal view of playwriting from Aeschylus to the present day, and *Changing Stages: A View of British Theatre in the Twentieth Century*, co-written with Richard Eyre.

THE LAST OF THE DUCHESS

Nicholas Wright

based on the book by
Caroline Blackwood

NICK HERN BOOKS
London
www.nickhernbooks.co.uk

A Nick Hern Book

The Last of the Duchess, based on the book by Caroline Blackwood, first published in 2011 by Nick Hern Books Limited, 14 Larden Road, London W3 7ST

The Last of the Duchess copyright © Somerset West Ltd, 2011
Based on the book copyright © the Estate of Caroline Blackwood

Nicholas Wright has asserted his right to be identified as the author of this work

Cover image: Getty Images
Cover design: Ned Hoste, 2H

Typeset by Nick Hern Books, London
Printed in the UK by Mimeo Ltd, St Ives, Cambs PE27 3LE

A CIP catalogue record for this book is available from the British Library

ISBN 978 1 84842 206 3

The Last of the Duchess was first performed at Hampstead Theatre, London, on 26 October 2011 (previews from 20 October), with the following cast:

LADY CAROLINE BLACKWOOD	Anna Chancellor
THE DUCHESS OF WINDSOR / TESSA	Helen Bradbury
MICHAEL BLOCH	John Heffernan
MAÎTRE SUZANNE BLUM	Sheila Hancock
GEORGES	Conrad Asquith
OFÉLIA	Jasmina Daniel
LADY MOSLEY	Angela Thorne

Director	Richard Eyre
Designer	Anthony Ward
Lighting Designer	Peter Mumford
Sound Designer	John Leonard
Casting Director	Cara Beckinsale CDG

Characters

in order of appearance

CAROLINE BLACKWOOD
THE DUCHESS OF WINDSOR
MICHAEL BLOCH
MAÎTRE SUZANNE BLUM
GEORGES, *a butler*
OFÉLIA, *Georges' wife, the housekeeper*
TESSA, *Lord Snowdon's assistant*
LADY MOSLEY

Place: the Windsors' house in the Bois de Boulogne, Paris

Time: 1980

*This text went to press before the end of rehearsals and so may
differ slightly from the play as performed.*

Scene One

Darkness.

Captions:

IN 1936,
EDWARD VIII, KING OF GREAT BRITAIN AND IRELAND
AND THE BRITISH DOMINIONS BEYOND THE SEAS
DEFENDER OF THE FAITH
AND EMPEROR OF INDIA,
ABDICATED IN ORDER TO MARRY WALLIS SIMPSON.
HE WAS CREATED DUKE OF WINDSOR.
HE DIED IN 1972.
THE DUCHESS LIVED ON.

CAROLINE BLACKWOOD *appears in the darkness.*

CAROLINE. The taxi pulls away. The rain is still bucketing
down. The house is surrounded by viciously spiked iron
railings and there's a pair of huge steel gates. I feel a moment
of dread but I suppress it. I ring the outside bell and
somebody buzzes the lock. As I walk up the drive, I notice
how neglected the grounds are. The lawn is growing waist-
high like an un-mown meadow, and there's an ornamental
tree with rings of repulsive yellow fungus around it. I wait at
the door. I remember how, when I was a child in County
Down, eyes were rolled and voices dropped to sepulchral
whispers whenever the Duchess of Windsor's name was
mentioned. Nobody told me why this was, so she quickly
became a figure of louche and seductive glamour in my eyes.
Whatever she'd done, it was something that my mother
considered unspeakable. I liked the sound of that at once!

There's a change of atmosphere.

Inside the house, the shutters are closed. The rooms are dark.
The salon is indescribably cold. She stands at the fireplace,
lighting the candles...

The DUCHESS OF WINDSOR *appears at the fireplace, one hand resting lightly on the mantelpiece. She is younger than you'd expect, crisp, lucid and manageably drunk.*

... wearing a plain black Mainbocher dress, a diamond brooch, pearl earrings and a pair of white kid gloves.

DUCHESS. You'll have a vodka?

CAROLINE. Thank you, I will.

The DUCHESS *pours a vodka.* CAROLINE *gets a pen and a blue exercise book out of her handbag. Meanwhile:*

I hope you won't mind if I write in my notebook while we're talking?

DUCHESS. Why would I mind? Go ahead, my dear! The *routine* in this house is that a first-time visitor will be offered a glass of chilled champagne *or* a whisky *or* the tiniest little vodka. I make a note of whatever you choose and, the next time you come, it will be presented to you on a silver tray by one of the footmen. Assuming there *is* a next time! I only invite amusing people.

CAROLINE. Yes, so I've heard.

The DUCHESS *gives* CAROLINE *an empty glass, keeping the one with vodka in it for herself.* CAROLINE *upends her glass, puzzled.*

This glass is empty!

DUCHESS. The arrival of the *hors d'oeuvres* is always a great event. I pay the closest attention to their appearance. Chefs are strangely blind when it comes to colour. Tiny bacon pieces frizzled with brown sugar, exactly the same as the Duke and I would have had served in the Bahamas. Fried mussels, grapes stuffed with cream cheese and cucumber sandwiches, with the thinnest possible bread and the cucumber cut in strips with the seeds removed. At 9:15 precisely, the butler announces, '*Son Altesse Royale est servie.*' 'Her Royal Highness'! That's me!

She laughs.

The Palace would fly into conniptions if they heard that '*Royale*', but what do I care? 'Fuck them and their banjo too,' as we say in Baltimore.

She takes CAROLINE*'s empty glass.*

My word, that didn't last long. Can I pour you another?

CAROLINE. You certainly can. Is there some reason why…?

The DUCHESS *interrupts while refilling her own glass.*

DUCHESS. The dining room is a profoundly deep and luminous Chinese blue. The lights are low and silvery. Nothing gold. Every fool knows that with tweeds and daywear, one wears whatever gold one has, but in the evening only platinum is acceptable. The Duke brought the silver from Buckingham Palace. It's magnificent, of course. Knives, forks and spoons in greater variety than you could shake a stick at. Here you are.

She hands CAROLINE*'s empty glass back to her.*

No soup to start with. After the cocktails, it's just more liquid sloshing down one's throat. Lobster mousse, perhaps, then chicken Maryland. Southern cooking, as the Negroes do it, is irresistible. Forgive my saying this, Caroline, but you're looking at me very strangely.

CAROLINE. Could I possibly have a vodka with some vodka in it?

DUCHESS. Why, of course.

She takes back CAROLINE*'s empty glass and refills her own.*

Is there anything else disturbing you?

CAROLINE. In fact there is.

DUCHESS. Do tell me.

CAROLINE. Everyone told me you were ill.

DUCHESS. Ill and ancient?

CAROLINE. Ancient as well.

DUCHESS. What about dying?

CAROLINE. Dying too. Or probably dying.

DUCHESS. Probably dying. Is that what they said? My so-called friends? Well, take a good look, my dear.

She preens.

I have the muscle tone of a greyhound and the waistline of an elf. I do my correspondence on the dot, I go to fashion shows, I entertain and I give interviews.

CAROLINE (*dismayed*). When did you last give an interview?

DUCHESS. Why, I've done three this week!

She laughs.

Oh, my poor girl! I hope you didn't imagine that I was granting you an *exclusive*?

CAROLINE. Yes, I did. I've come all the way from London exactly for that reason.

DUCHESS. Don't get stressed. I'm sure that your charming editor will understand. Now close your eyes and think of beautiful things. Rubies are beautiful. They're rich and luscious. Emeralds are cold and poisonous. Pearls are the colour of death.

She disappears. MICHAEL BLOCH*'s voice is heard:*

MICHAEL. Lady Caroline?

CAROLINE *wakes with a terrified gasp, as from a nightmare.* MICHAEL *is there. He's a nice-looking, demure young man of twenty-five or so, dressed in a striped boating jacket. It's late afternoon in the salon in the Windsor mansion in the Bois de Boulogne. It is grand in concept and busy with pictures, antique furniture and ornaments but faded and depressing. A pair of big double doors, a door to the study and French windows looking onto an untended garden.*

CAROLINE. Who are you?

MICHAEL. I'm Michael Bloch. Nothing's wrong. You were asleep, that's all.

CAROLINE. Jesus Christ, you gave me a fright. Don't *jump* on people.

MICHAEL. Sorry about that! But I really did have to wake you. My master will be here in a couple of minutes.

CAROLINE. Who's your master?

MICHAEL. Maître Blum, of course! I'm her assistant. She's my tutor at the Paris bar. My 'pupil-master'! Hence the appellation. You'll want this, I suppose.

He hands over her tape recorder. She starts setting it up with difficulty.

You'll find my master a very remarkable woman for her age. She walks as fast as most people run. And did you know that she still practises as a lawyer? I'm living in a tiny garret in her office. It's up some winding stairs with a view over the Paris rooftops. It's very romantic. It's like being in *La Bohème.*

He laughs. She's struggling with the tape recorder.

Are you all right with that?

CAROLINE (*in despair*). No, the batteries are all the wrong size!

MICHAEL. Give it to me.

He takes it and fiddles with the batteries.

Would you mind if I gave you some advice? Don't ask her about the Duchess's state of health. It's bound to put her in a rage. And whatever you do, don't mention the Queen Mother. I once said something vaguely nice about her, and her reaction was volcanic.

He's sorted out the tape recorder.

Here you are. She'll be along in a moment.

He leaves. CAROLINE *prepares for the interview. In a snap of anxiety she looks beside her for the blue exercise book, but of course it isn't there. She takes it out of her handbag. Presses the 'record' button on the tape recorder.*

CAROLINE. Interview Maître Blum, April 15th, 1980.

She plays a bit of it back. Takes a half-bottle of Stoli out of her bag, drinks and puts it back. Takes out a packet of cigarettes, takes one out and is about to light it. The big doors fly open and MAÎTRE SUZANNE BLUM *is there: an austerely handsome woman with fashionably cut white hair. She speaks briskly, in excellent English. She is carrying a book.*

MAÎTRE BLUM (*with vehemence*). Don't smoke!

She gestures towards her eyes: the smoke affects them.

My eyes.

She volleys into the room at amazing speed, followed by MICHAEL.

(*To* MICHAEL.) *Michael, vous resterez ici pendant la durée de l'interview, comme convenu. Mais avant tout, j'ai une instruction pour vous.*

She produces a large bunch of keys and moves towards an escritoire.

CAROLINE. If you're going to talk, I may as well smoke outside.

MAÎTRE BLUM. Don't take too long.

She sighs and unlocks one of the French windows. CAROLINE *collects her handbag as a matter of urgency and goes out.*

(*To* MICHAEL.) This is a very fine interview you have persuaded me to give. Her shoes are unpolished and her blouse is crumpled. Now listen closely.

She produces the book she came in with.

This is Lady Mosley's new biography of the Duchess.

MICHAEL. What's it like?

MAÎTRE BLUM. Don't interrupt! On page 112, I find a photograph of the Duchess reproduced with no permission from me, and what is worse is that I have received no fee. When this interview is over, which will be very soon, you will telephone the publisher, Lord Longford, and demand four hundred English pounds.

MICHAEL. Have we the rights of the photograph?

MAÎTRE BLUM. Michael, you are a sweet and delightful boy, but you must learn to pay attention. Long Longford must pay four hundred pounds to the estate of the Duchess, or I will serve an injunction on this book that has already been printed! *Now* do you understand?

MICHAEL *nods.*

Good.

She goes to an escritoire and takes out a bundle of letters. Meanwhile:

What is she doing?

MICHAEL *looks out into the garden and tells a half-truth.*

MICHAEL. She's smoking.

MAÎTRE BLUM *shakes her head at this folly, selects a letter and peers at it through her spectacles.*

MAÎTRE BLUM. This letter contains a unique comment by the Duke, sent to the Duchess on the 14th of May 1943, while she was in Miami for a wisdom tooth extraction. You will find it indispensable for your book.

MICHAEL. Thank you.

MAÎTRE BLUM. When you have photocopied it, you will return the original. *Oh la la,* I can't put this off any longer.

She bangs on the windowpane and beckons for CAROLINE *to come in.* MICHAEL *is about to take a seat with its back to a window. She indicates another chair.*

No, no! Sit there!

CAROLINE *comes back in.*

CAROLINE. I threw my cigarette into the brambles. I hope that's all right?

MAÎTRE BLUM. You may sit.

She indicates the chair that MICHAEL *first tried.*
CAROLINE *sits and discovers that the late-afternoon light from the window is shining directly in her eyes. She opens her notebook.*

Michael, you will make a note of every word that passes between us.

MICHAEL *gets out whatever he needs.*

Young Mr Bloch is your compatriot, Lady Caroline. He comes from the north of Ireland. Both of you come from the United Kingdom's worst trouble spot.

CAROLINE (*pleasantly*). Well, I hope I won't be too much trouble to you today. Oh, and thank you so much for agreeing to meet me. I've been greatly looking forward to it.

MAÎTRE BLUM. I could not meet you on the date that you first proposed. I was *en voiture.*

MICHAEL. Madame was 'on the road'.

CAROLINE (*politely*). Oh, is that so?

MAÎTRE BLUM. I have been travelling many times between my apartment in Paris and my country home.

MICHAEL. Madame's husband, the General, is gravely ill.

CAROLINE. Oh, I'm sorry to hear that. Which part of the country is he…?

MICHAEL. We've moved him to Paris. He's in the American Hospital.

MAÎTRE BLUM. Too much *explication*, Michael!

CAROLINE. Shall I turn this on?

She means her tape recorder. MAÎTRE BLUM *gives a dismissive shrug.* CAROLINE *turns it on.*

As I said in my letter to you, Maître Blum, I've been commissioned by Mr Francis Wyndham of the *Sunday Times* colour supplement, to write a profile of… Her Royal Highness the Duchess of Windsor. I know that you are her lawyer, and I…

MAÎTRE BLUM. *Je suis la défenseur des droits moraux et des intérêts de la Duchesse de Windsor.*

CAROLINE. So that all communications with her...

MAÎTRE BLUM. ... must go...

CAROLINE. ... through you, exactly.

MAÎTRE BLUM. That is correct.

CAROLINE. Of course, we're terribly disappointed that she won't be available for an interview.

MAÎTRE BLUM. I'm sure you are.

CAROLINE. Is that quite definite?

MAÎTRE BLUM. Yes.

CAROLINE. So may I ask you some questions about her?

MAÎTRE BLUM. You may. But I am *not* to be quoted. *Never.*

CAROLINE. I don't know that I can promise that. Whatever I write will have to be attributed to someone or other.

MAÎTRE BLUM. You are mistaken. If it is not attributed it will be more interesting.

A crafty smile:

People will have to guess who you've been talking to. It will be a nice little puzzle for them.

CAROLINE. Well, we can talk about that later.

MAÎTRE BLUM. I don't think so.

She raises her eyebrows at MICHAEL. CAROLINE *consults her exercise book.*

CAROLINE. To start with, why don't you tell me about the Windsors? What were they like?

MAÎTRE BLUM. They were exceptional people. It was a privilege to be their friend. They were highly... cultivated. Is that how you say it in English?

CAROLINE. Cultured?

MAÎTRE BLUM. They were very cultured. They liked to stay at home and read good books and listen to classical music. I remember those evenings very well. I would sit in that chair where you sit now, the Duke was there…

She indicates another chair, then moves swiftly over to the fireplace.

… and the Duchess would stand here at the fireplace, one hand resting on the, the…

She taps the mantelpiece.

CAROLINE. … the chimney piece.

MAÎTRE BLUM (*doubtfully*). Exactly. If the Duke went to bed early, as sometimes happened after a tiring day at the golf course, the Duchess and I would discuss artistic matters or the international situation.

CAROLINE. Are you still very close to the Duchess?

MAÎTRE BLUM. We have *une relation chaleureuse.*

MICHAEL (*quietly to* CAROLINE). '*Chaleureuse*' means 'warm'.

CAROLINE. Yes, I know *that*, but…

MAÎTRE BLUM. It's an *affectionate* relationship. The last time that the Duchess went out in public, she dined in my apartment in the Rue de Varenne.

CAROLINE. That must have been great fun for her.

MAÎTRE BLUM. We *both* had fun. I quite understood why the Duke fell so in love with her.

CAROLINE *perks up with interest.*

CAROLINE. Oh, did you? What is her most attractive quality, do you think?

MAÎTRE BLUM. She is dignified. Immensely dignified. And highly intelligent. Both of them were. The Duke had one of the finest legal minds of his generation.

CAROLINE. Really?

MAÎTRE BLUM. Oh yes. Whenever I submitted a document to him, I was amazed by how he always picked out the vital clause. And he was kind to the point of self-sacrifice.

CAROLINE. In what way?

MAÎTRE BLUM. He would open the doors of cars for people of no importance.

Pause.

CAROLINE. Anything else?

MAÎTRE BLUM. He cared about sick animals and orphans. His charity budget was enormous. Both the Windsors wished only to do good works and make life better for the poor.

CAROLINE. I don't think I've ever come across that piece of information.

MAÎTRE BLUM. Of course you have not! They did not boast about it. They didn't want anyone to know how much they spent on hospitals and homes for orphans. They kept it secret, otherwise they would have been drowned in begging letters.

CAROLINE. Well, on the subject of their generosity… it's sometimes said…

She gets out a newspaper cutting.

MAÎTRE BLUM. In a filthy newspaper?

CAROLINE. … it says… yes, here… that the Windsors found it difficult to tip.

MAÎTRE BLUM. To *tip*? To *tip*?

She makes up-ending gestures in the air.

Why would the Duchess want to *tip*? Do you think that she is an acrobat? You are insulting her! You are a jackal!

CAROLINE (*annoyed*). I didn't mean tipping *upside down*…!

MICHAEL. Lady Caroline is referring to giving small sums of money to the…

CAROLINE. . . . yes, like a bellboy lugging eighty-four huge pieces of luggage to the top floor of the Waldorf Astoria, and the Duke fishing in his pocket and coming up with *fifty cents*. Oh, look, forget the question.

MAÎTRE BLUM. I have forgotten it already.

CAROLINE. But isn't it true that they led a rather pointless existence?

MAÎTRE BLUM. 'Pointless' how?

CAROLINE. Well, weren't they both obsessed with dinner parties and buying clothes and doing up houses?

MAÎTRE BLUM. Slanderous lies!

CAROLINE. The stories about their dancing in nightclubs till the crack of dawn. They're all invented, are they?

MAÎTRE BLUM. The Duchess never went to nightclubs!

CAROLINE. I've also heard that she drank a lot.

MAÎTRE BLUM. She never drank.

CAROLINE. What, not at all?

MAÎTRE BLUM *indicates a thimble-sized measure.*

MAÎTRE BLUM. The Duchess drank maybe *this* much, once or twice in her life. And only because it was offered to her. *Par politesse*, you understand. She was always polite. But I will tell you something that nobody knows.

CAROLINE. Yes?

MAÎTRE BLUM. The trouble was not that the Duchess drank, but that she never ate.

CAROLINE. She was anorexic?

MAÎTRE BLUM. It was the slimming. Always slimming. She took a nibble from an apple here, a biscuit there. She strived always for perfection of her appearance. Not out of vanity, no, no, no. It was to elevate the lives of the people around her.

CAROLINE. Is that why she had so many facelifts?

MAÎTRE BLUM *stares at her, angry and suspicious.*

MAÎTRE BLUM. How should I know about facelifts? I am only her lawyer.

She rises and presses a service bell.

Now you can write your article for the *Sunday Times*. I must read it before it is published. I may wish to rewrite it.

CAROLINE. Was that the interview?

MAÎTRE BLUM. It's all I will give you. Why should I help my client's enemies to spatter her with *ordure*?

MICHAEL (*helpfully*). '*Ordure*' means...

CAROLINE. 'Shit'! I know.

MAÎTRE BLUM. My mission in life is to prove that their lies are lies. I've done so many times. I have won abject apologies and most handsome sums of money on her behalf. Your editor would do well to remember that.

CAROLINE. Well, if you can't trust me to tell the truth...

MAÎTRE BLUM. Why would I *trust* you? People lie in the newspapers. They lie in books. There's not one book been published that is not *ragot de cuisine*. That is not *dégoûtant*! I despise them all!

GEORGES, *the butler, appears. About sixty-five, short dark jacket, grey trousers.*

Georges, telephone for a taxi for Lady Caroline. She is leaving.

GEORGES. Madame.

He backs out. MAÎTRE BLUM *collects her things.*

MAÎTRE BLUM. I must go upstairs to visit Her Royal Highness. Lady Caroline, you will ensure that your article is given the prominence my client deserves. How long will it be?

CAROLINE. My editor wants a thousand words...

MAÎTRE BLUM. Too short.

CAROLINE. ... and the opposite page would be entirely taken up by the photograph.

MAÎTRE BLUM. What photograph?

CAROLINE. Lord Snowdon... I'm sure you've heard of him... would very much like to take a portrait of the Duchess. And the piece that I write will accompany it. In the *Sunday Times*.

   MAÎTRE BLUM *stares at her suspiciously.*

MAÎTRE BLUM. This is Lord Snowdon who married the Princess Margaret?

CAROLINE. He *was* married to her, but then it all got a bit tricky.

MAÎTRE BLUM. Is his interest definite?

CAROLINE. Yes, he's very keen. He's a brilliant photographer too.

MAÎTRE BLUM. Except his style, I remember now, is *très moderne*. He will show every line of exhaustion, every dark spot of age on the hands.

   She glances at her hands and puts them out of sight.

CAROLINE. No, no, that's not what he wants at all. He wants to show the Duchess as, not *youthful*, of course, but serene and timeless. A woman who's risen above the obstacles of her life to become an example to the whole world. A woman worthy of being a queen. Do you think the Duchess would have made a good queen?

MAÎTRE BLUM. Oh yes! She would have been a wonderful queen!

   She settles back into a chair.

   It is possible, Lady Caroline, that I have not been sufficiently helpful to you. I have always to be *sur mes gardes* to ensure my client's safety. Everything written up till now has been malicious tittle-tattle. Only when lazy Michael writes his book will the truth be told.

   CAROLINE *glances at* LADY MOSLEY*'s book.*

CAROLINE. What about Lady Mosley's book? I hear it's fantastically nice about the Duchess.

MAÎTRE BLUM. It says nothing new. It is a book *sans couleur, sans odeur et sans saveur.* I am surprised that a woman of such noble ancestry could not do better. Perhaps she is losing her mind. She behaved very strangely when she came to this house last month. I had to summon Georges to remove her.

CAROLINE. Well, that brings me to a very important question.

MAÎTRE BLUM. Which is what?

CAROLINE. What is the Duchess's state of health?

  MAÎTRE BLUM *controls herself.*

MAÎTRE BLUM. She is not well. But she is not in any danger. Dr Thin is not worried about her.

CAROLINE. Dr Tan? Is he Chinese?

MICHAEL (*quietly*). T – H – I – N.

CAROLINE. Thin?

  She twigs that the name is French, and writes it down.

  Oh, '*Thin*'. Do you mind my writing that she is ill?

MAÎTRE BLUM. No! Don't write that!

CAROLINE. But I've got to say *something*. How else can I explain why she never appears in public?

MAÎTRE BLUM. She doesn't parade herself. Why should she?

CAROLINE. But that doesn't explain why she never goes out at all.

  MICHAEL *speaks quietly to* MAÎTRE BLUM.

MICHAEL. It would seem a little odd, *mon maître*, if there weren't even the smallest reference to the Duchess's health.

  MAÎTRE BLUM *sighs regretfully.*

MAÎTRE BLUM. *Michael a raison.* I'm afraid you had better say that she is ill.

CAROLINE. Can she speak?

MAÎTRE BLUM. Of course she speaks!

CAROLINE. I'm sure the readers will be very happy to hear that. How often does she speak?

MAÎTRE BLUM. Every day!

CAROLINE. Can you give an example of the kind of thing she says?

MAÎTRE BLUM. She says 'Good morning'…

CAROLINE *waits.*

… and 'Good evening.' Now I've nothing else to say.

CAROLINE. How often does Dr – Dr Thin come to see her?

MAÎTRE BLUM. She has many doctors.

CAROLINE. And nurses too?

MAÎTRE BLUM. She has many nurses.

CAROLINE. So I suppose her medical expenses must be… well, I imagine they're quite heavy?

MAÎTRE BLUM. Her expenses?

She raises her voice and gestures extravagantly.

Ils sont exorbitants! Ils sont terribles! Ils sont affreux!

MICHAEL (*helpfully*). Very heavy indeed.

(*Embarrassedly to* CAROLINE.) Sorry.

CAROLINE. But that shouldn't be too difficult for her, should it? Weren't the Duke and the Duchess very rich?

MAÎTRE BLUM. They were never rich.

CAROLINE. They must have been *quite* rich. Didn't the Duke get a big allowance from the Civil List? And he inherited a huge fortune, and they didn't even have to pay for this house because it was lent to them by the French Government.

MAÎTRE BLUM. They did great services for France.

CAROLINE. Besides, the Duchess used to spend a hundred thousand dollars a year on clothes.

MAÎTRE BLUM. It was her sacrifice for him.

CAROLINE. What about her jewels?

MAÎTRE BLUM. Her *what*?

CAROLINE. Her jewels. The one thing that the Duchess was most famous for...

MAÎTRE BLUM. *Was? Was?*

CAROLINE. ... apart from her clothes and her facelifts...

MAÎTRE BLUM. Lies! All lies!

CAROLINE. ... was, is her jewel collection. All those priceless Victorian pieces that she had chopped up and turned into panthers and parrots and teddy bears...

MAÎTRE BLUM *laughs in derision.*

MAÎTRE BLUM. Such fantasies!

CAROLINE. ... and a lot of the jewels that she got off the Duke belonged to Queen Alexandra...

MAÎTRE BLUM. The Duchess has *nothing* of Queen Alexandra's! Not one seed pearl!

CAROLINE. Well, even if that's true, it wouldn't hurt her to sell off a necklace or two. It's not as though she gets very much chance to wear them.

MAÎTRE BLUM. The Duchess would rather sell her heart, than a jewel from a man who gave up the throne of England for her sake.

CAROLINE. Well, speaking of thrones of England...

MICHAEL *signals 'Stop right there!'*

... if she's really so desperately hard up, can't the Royal Family help her? They're rolling in money. Or don't they care about her?

MAÎTRE BLUM *replies with tact.*

MAÎTRE BLUM. The Royal Family has been most gracious. They send Christmas cards and birthday congratulations.

She gets out her watch and affects surprise at the time.

Oh! I am late. Michael, go to the study and telephone Lord Longford. At once! Why do you walk so slow like an old peasant behind a donkey cart? *Vite, vite!*

MICHAEL *goes via the smaller door to the study.*

CAROLINE (*with determination*). And when the Duchess dies…?

MAÎTRE BLUM. Don't you dare to speak that word!

CAROLINE. But I have to ask you. When the Duchess passes away…

MAÎTRE BLUM. Don't say it!

CAROLINE. … will she be taken to England and be buried beside the Duke in the royal burial ground at Frogmore?

MAÎTRE BLUM. You must write nothing on that subject. If you do, your profile will never appear.

She rises to her feet.

You may wait in this salon until your taxi arrives. Good afternoon.

CAROLINE. But, Maître Blum…

MAÎTRE BLUM. I am exhausted. You've worn me out.

CAROLINE. What about the photo?

MAÎTRE BLUM. What photo?

CAROLINE. The one I've just told you about. What I really do need to know… and so will my editor… because you seem quite unable to tell me… is whether the Duchess is well enough to be photographed by Lord Snowdon?

MAÎTRE BLUM *considers for a moment. Then:*

MAÎTRE BLUM. There are advantages and disadvantages. It is essential that nothing too stressful occurs to affect her heart and lungs. I shall reflect on this. Michael will telephone you with my decision. And there is something of great importance that I must add. If your article is not favourable to the Duchess...

CAROLINE. ... then you'll sue the paper, yes I know.

MAÎTRE BLUM. No, I will not sue the *Sunday Times*. I will not sue you either.

She smiles thinly and says with conviction, though not loudly:

I will *keel* you.

She goes out via the big doors, leaving CAROLINE *stunned.*

CAROLINE. Bloody hell.

GEORGES *comes in.*

GEORGES. Lady Caroline's taxi is at the gate.

CAROLINE. I'll be down in a minute.

She glances at GEORGES *and he goes. She gets the half-bottle out of her handbag and takes a couple of swallows.* MICHAEL *comes in from the study, holding the Duke of Windsor's letter.*

MICHAEL. Are you all right?

CAROLINE. No, I'm not. She threatened to kill me.

MICHAEL. She wasn't serious.

CAROLINE. You weren't here.

MICHAEL. I know what she's like! She always plays up the drama. I saw her once in court, when she was acting for a dancer who was suing the Paris Ballet because she'd been dropped on the floor in the middle of *Swan Lake. Mon maître* raised her arms in the air as though she was acting in Racine, and she declaimed to the skies, 'My client has been let down in every sense of the word!'

He laughs.

CAROLINE. I can't think why she agreed to see me.

MICHAEL. It was the handle. She loves a title, *Lady* Caroline!

CAROLINE. So she invited me here because she's a howling snob. And then she called me a jackal and told me a pack of lies.

MICHAEL. Not lies exactly.

CAROLINE. Tactical evasions?

MICHAEL. You could put it like that.

CAROLINE. What's she evading?

MICHAEL. I don't know.

She stares at him, wondering whether or not to believe him.

CAROLINE. What's this book she says you're writing?

MICHAEL. Oh, that! It's about the Duke and Duchess during the war, when he was Governor of the Bahamas.

CAROLINE. Hasn't that been done?

MICHAEL. Well, yes it has, but dreadfully badly. She's giving me lots of new material.

CAROLINE. What sort of material?

MICHAEL. Letters that they wrote to each other. She says that some of them are very lovey-dovey. She was digging this one out for me while you were drinking in the garden.

He stops.

Oops. Sorry.

Embarrassed, he looks at the letter.

This one isn't lovey-dovey at all. It's just the Duke complaining about his job. He had good reason to, of course. He could have done lots more for the war effort, if only Winston Churchill had let him. You can look at it if you like.

He gives CAROLINE *the letter. She glances at it and hands it back.*

Should I be doing something about your taxi?

CAROLINE. It's arrived.

MICHAEL. Well, I hope we'll stay in touch.

CAROLINE. We will. She wants you to tell me whether or not there'll be a photograph.

MICHAEL. Will they still print your article if there isn't?

CAROLINE. There won't *be* an article.

MICHAEL. Why not?

CAROLINE. Because I've got nothing to *put* in it that any sane person would *believe*!

She buries her head in her hands.

Oh, God!

MICHAEL. Well, don't give up.

CAROLINE. Why not?

MICHAEL. It'd be so nice to know you were coming back. I'm a tremendous fan of yours. I love your books.

CAROLINE. You've read them?

MICHAEL. Yes, of course.

CAROLINE. Which ones?

MICHAEL. All of them. I like *Great Granny Webster* the most. I tried to get Maître Blum to read it, but she threw it across the room. She said it showed a macabre view of human nature.

CAROLINE. It's news to me there's any other view.

MICHAEL. Is that really what happened at the cemetery? Did the old one-eyed woman really get blinded by the funeral ashes?

CAROLINE. It's a novel, okay?

MICHAEL. It's mostly true, though, isn't it? The crumbling Irish mansion with the leaks in the roof dripping down lengths of string into the buckets. And the drunken servants and the terrible food. Isn't that Clandeboye? It's wonderfully captured in the book. Of course, I've only seen it from across the lake.

CAROLINE. You've seen it?

MICHAEL. Yes, my father used to point it out when we were driving to the seaside. Or we'd picnic there. There's a wonderful view of the house from the shore of the lake. It looks quite magical. And there'd be people swimming and laughing over on the other side. My father would say, 'That's where the Dufferin and Ava's live, the family that the yacht race is named after.' We were living in County Armagh, so we weren't very far away from you, geographically speaking. In every other way, of course, we lived in a different world.

CAROLINE. I wouldn't have known you came from there, if she hadn't told me.

MICHAEL. Oh, I never had an accent. Not even when I first started to talk. I suppose it didn't fit in with the way that I imagined my life working out.

CAROLINE. What a strange young man you are.

MICHAEL. Quite a few people have told me that.

CAROLINE. Are you in Paris on your own?

MICHAEL. Completely, yes.

CAROLINE. Then why are you wasting your time with that old monster? Let alone in that ridiculous jacket.

MICHAEL. Don't you like it?

CAROLINE. No, I don't. It makes you look like a chorus boy in *Salad Days*. Grow up, for God's sake! You ought to be out on the town, fucking your brains out.

MICHAEL. I do try.

CAROLINE. Well, ditch the jacket.

MICHAEL. All right, I will.

He takes off his jacket. Laughs pleasantly, as though taking it off has freed him.

How's that?

CAROLINE. Much better.

MICHAEL. I've been upstairs.

CAROLINE. *Here?* My *God*! How totally *terrifying*. What's it like?

MICHAEL. The same as down here. Vulgar and sad and sort of tarnished. It gave me the creeps. There was a gold pen on the Duke's writing desk that looked as though he'd put it there five minutes ago, but you could tell by the dust that it hadn't been moved for ages.

CAROLINE. And?

MICHAEL. There was a long dark corridor, and the Duchess's suite was at the far end. Like a chrysalis at the end of a tunnel. Except a chrysalis is the *start* of life, and this was the end of life. It was like the shrine of some long-dead Saint with a few old bones piled up in a velvet casket. There was a light under the door, and I could hear a couple of nurses talking quietly in Spanish.

CAROLINE. Did you see the Duchess?

MICHAEL. No, that'd be more than my life is worth!

He glances at the Duke's letter.

I'm not just cosying up to her in order to get research material. I like her. I find her captivating. I've got a very soft spot for difficult women. They're so much more interesting than the other kind.

CAROLINE. Oh, yes?

MICHAEL. I haven't just read your books. I've seen Lucian Freud's paintings of you too. Some of them in reproduction and then the one in the exhibition at the Hayward a couple of years ago. *Girl in Bed.* That's his early masterpiece, don't you think?

CAROLINE. It's one of the two or three. He painted it here in Paris, right over the market in the Rue de Seine. There's a look in my eyes that always surprises me. He must have seen it in me, though I doubt it was really there. Puzzled and babyish… and ancient and wise… all at the same time. We slept on the floor for weeks, because we couldn't unrumple the sheets until he'd finished. I was twenty-one. We'd just eloped.

MICHAEL. At least you can't be accused of marrying dull men.

CAROLINE. No, I can't.

MICHAEL. Then you married the composer. Then the poet. How long is it since the poet died?

CAROLINE. Two years and seven months. Just leave it, will you?

MICHAEL. Sorry.

GEORGES *comes in.*

GEORGES. Madame's taxi-driver wishes to know if he's still required.

CAROLINE (*to* MICHAEL). I can give you a lift if you want.

MICHAEL. I've got my bike. Goodnight.

CAROLINE. Goodnight.

MICHAEL *goes.*

CAROLINE (*to* GEORGES). Georges?

GEORGES. Madame?

CAROLINE. I understand that Lady Mosley came here last month.

GEORGES (*with reverence*). Lady Mosley visits every month. She stays for an hour or more and we speak together about the Duchess's health and happiness.

CAROLINE. Just you and her?

GEORGES *frowns: what's the point of the question?*

You see, what I don't understand is why Lady Mosley couldn't go upstairs and talk to the Duchess face to face? Or hold her hand or just sit next to her, if she's not in a state to talk. Isn't that the kind of thing that old people enjoy?

GEORGES. Madame?

CAROLINE. Has Maître Blum ordered you not to let anyone see the Duchess? Not even her oldest friends?

GEORGES. I cannot say. I am only the butler.

CAROLINE. Tell the taxi I'm on my way.

GEORGES *goes. It's now quite dark in the salon.*
CAROLINE *has another vodka. Turns on her tape recorder.*
Records:

Once upon a time there was a woman who was loved so much by a king that he gave up his throne for her. She wore jewels and gave parties and played music and danced all night, but then her husband died and she was suddenly very old. Now she lay in bed in a long half-dream, in a darkened palace barred with an iron gate and surrounded by brambles. She had been captured by a demon. And nobody knew why the demon was keeping her all to herself. That was her secret.

Through the big doors, MAÎTRE BLUM *and* MICHAEL *can be heard talking outside.* CAROLINE *stops and listens.*

MAÎTRE BLUM. *Michael, avez-vous téléphoné à Lord Longford?*

MICHAEL. *Oui, madame.*

MAÎTRE BLUM. *Qu'a-t-il dit? A-t-il accepté nos exigences? Ne restez pas planté là! Racontez-moi!*

MICHAEL. *Oui, il a accepté, madame, mais il n'était pas très content.*

MAÎTRE BLUM. *Tant qu'il a accepté! C'est tout ce qui compte!*

MAÎTRE BLUM *is heard chuckling gleefully: something that hasn't been heard before. She comes into the darkened room, not seeing that* CAROLINE *is there. She locks the escritoire, turns, sees* CAROLINE *and gasps in alarm.*

You frightened me!

CAROLINE. I'm sorry.

MAÎTRE BLUM. Has your taxi not arrived?

CAROLINE. It's waiting.

MAÎTRE BLUM. I've been considering your request.

CAROLINE. And?

MAÎTRE BLUM. The Duchess has been famous for many
decades. Or notorious, if you prefer. She has been called a
marriage-breaker, a usurper, an adventuress. She has been
called a devoted wife, a leader of fashion, a wit. There are
ten thousand photographs of her. They show her composed,
radiant, subdued with many cares. Which of these many
images is the Duchess?

She raises a finger in courtroom mode.

Not one! Humanity is profound. It is unknowable. It cannot
be captured... *captured*... by a picture in black and white, or
some words on a page. These are mere fragments of the
whole. There is no truth that you can write, or that Lord
Snowdon can portray, that can convey the woman I know, in
all her fullness and complexity. Your so-called truths will
only diminish her. And a human being must never be
diminished. Because a human being is sacred. So it will not
be possible for Lord Snowdon to photograph the Duchess.
You will tell your editor.

CAROLINE. Oh, I will.

*She puts her things together and is about to go when a
thought occurs to her.*

Although, I wonder... though he'd have to agree...

MAÎTRE BLUM. Agree to what?

CAROLINE. How would it be if Lord Snowdon photographed
you instead?

MAÎTRE BLUM *stares at her, astonished.*

MAÎTRE BLUM. Why me?

CAROLINE. If my profile was about *you*... and all the
fascinating things that you do for the Duchess... then I'm
quite sure that the *Sunday Times* would want to print it.

MAÎTRE BLUM. With a photograph by Lord Snowdon?

CAROLINE. Yes, I'm sure that could be arranged.

After a moment:

MAÎTRE BLUM (*graciously*). I will be happy to give permission.

She gestures a courteous dismissal.

Goodnight, Lady Caroline.

CAROLINE. Goodnight.

She goes out through the double doors. MAÎTRE BLUM *waits until the doors have closed. Then she moves quickly to the fireplace and looks earnestly at herself in the mirror. After a few moments, she turns and stands, one hand resting lightly on the mantelpiece, just as the* DUCHESS *did at the start of the play.*

End of Scene One.

Scene Two

The salon. A month or two later, mid-morning. TESSA, *Lord Snowdon's assistant, an attractive woman in her twenties, is collecting a photographer's lamp and other equipment, which she will take through the smaller door towards the study.* MICHAEL *watches.* CAROLINE *sits some distance away from the others, an overnight bag at her feet, making notes in her blue exercise book.*

MICHAEL. Excuse me!

TESSA. What?

MICHAEL. Will you be using that big lamp?

TESSA. I've no idea. And I think I ought to tell you that Lord Snowdon really isn't taking kindly to your suggestions about his lighting.

MICHAEL. I was only trying to help.

TESSA. Well, he's very annoyed and if you can't keep quiet you're jolly well going to have to stay out here.

MAÎTRE BLUM *comes in from the study. She's wearing a long gown and is lightly made up.* OFÉLIA, *the maid, about sixty years old, follows her in and they move quickly towards an improvised dressing table, where* MAÎTRE BLUM *checks her appearance and changes her earrings.*

MAÎTRE BLUM. What a charming man Lord Snowdon is! *Il est absolument délicieux! Très très très gentil.* But he doesn't approve these earrings. In any event, they are pinching me. I have not worn them for twenty years.

She considers another pair.

TESSA. We're not having a break, you know. We're just setting up with the bookcase in the background.

MICHAEL (*of the earrings*). Not the garnets.

MAÎTRE BLUM. Why?

MICHAEL. Too morbid.

MAÎTRE BLUM. You're right. I'm not an old widow yet. *Ofélia, essayons les boucles d'oreilles avec les perles. Non, pas cette camelote. Les autres.*

GEORGES *comes in through the big doors.*

TESSA. Can I just say that Lord Snowdon's plane is at three o'clock, and he can't stay in Paris a moment longer?

MAÎTRE BLUM (*to* MICHAEL). Every time this woman says they are ready to start. And then I wait and wait until my circulation has come to an 'alt.

CAROLINE (*to* TESSA, *who is on her way out*). Can I come and watch? I've finished my notes.

TESSA. Oh, you'll be welcome any old time, don't bother to ask. I've been meaning to tell you, I was at a party of your brother's the other day. He's such a sweetie, I do love him.

CAROLINE. Yes, so do I.

TESSA *goes.*

MAÎTRE BLUM (*to* MICHAEL). She is his mistress, I suppose.

With a meaningful glance at CAROLINE:

Still, it's nice to see an Englishwoman who takes care over her appearance.

GEORGES. *Madame, si je puis me permettre…?*

MAÎTRE BLUM. *Georges, que voulez-vous? Pourquoi n'êtes-vous pas auprés de notre bon Lord?*

GEORGES. *Avec votre permission, une affaire mineure mais urgente nécessite la presence d'Ofélia.*

MAÎTRE BLUM. *Plus tard, plus tard! Oh soit, faites comme vous voulez!*

OFÉLIA *proceeds towards the door.* MAÎTRE BLUM *holds the earrings in place.*

Michael, you are not looking. What's your opinion? Are these earrings too *fastueuses*? My English has flown out of the window.

MICHAEL. They're very dignified.

MAÎTRE BLUM *looks round in annoyance as* OFÉLIA *disappears.*

MAÎTRE BLUM. *Ofélia! Ou allez-vous? J'ai besoin d'aide!*

As she puts in her earrings herself.

She's been overexcited all day. It's her sixtieth birthday. My God, if I had looked like her when *I* was sixty, what would I look like now?

She examines her appearance.

Yes, these will do.

She stands.

Lady Caroline, when Lord Snowdon has finished, you may ask me the questions for your profile of me. I will have little to tell you. Very little indeed.

MAÎTRE BLUM, MICHAEL *and* GEORGES *go out.* CAROLINE *follows, leaving her handbag behind.*

The big doors open a tidge and OFÉLIA *peeps in. She opens the door wider and, with great respect, shows in a beautiful white-haired woman of seventy. This is* LADY MOSLEY.

LADY MOSLEY. *Ofélia, dites à Georges que je dois lui parler en privé. Et pouvez-vous m'apporter un verre d'eau?*

OFÉLIA. *Tout de suite, madame.*

OFÉLIA *goes. The small door opens.* CAROLINE *comes in and makes a beeline for her handbag. Seeing* LADY MOSLEY, *she stops as one caught out.*

CAROLINE. Oh, hello, Diana.

LADY MOSLEY. Goodness, Caroline.

CAROLINE. What're you doing here?

LADY MOSLEY. I've come to speak to Georges. It's really very important. I'd no idea that all this would be going on. Is that horrible old woman really here?

CAROLINE. Snowdon's photographing her in the study.

LADY MOSLEY. Yes, Ofélia told me. Have they just begun?

CAROLINE. No, they'll be finished pretty soon.

LADY MOSLEY (*who is deaf*). Until this afternoon? Good, then I'll be out of the house before they finish. I cannot meet her, I really can't. We had the most frightful bust-up last time we met.

She sits and checks the contents of her handbag.

CAROLINE. You could come back when she isn't here.

LADY MOSLEY. You'll have to say that again when my head's not buried in my handbag. I had something very valuable inside and it seems to have gorn.

She's found it.

No, it was hiding. Caroline, I'm so sorry I couldn't talk when you telephoned me last week. The dogs were barking like mad things. And I've had too much on my mind to telephone you back. Sir Oz is very much worse.

CAROLINE. Oh, what's wrong with him now?

LADY MOSLEY. What *isn't* wrong? He's eighty-four. He's falling to bits.

CAROLINE is about to sit next to her.

No, sit on this side. I'm deaf as a post on the other one. It's too dreary for all words. People say, 'Oh, isn't it wonderful that Lady Mosley still goes to parties,' but what's the point, if all I can do is sit in a corner with a sickly grin on my face nodding like a yo-yo? Have you been in Paris long?

CAROLINE. No, I've just got off the plane.

LADY MOSLEY. Where are you staying?

CAROLINE. I've found a wonderful *maison de passe* in Place Pigalle. It's incredibly cheap, the girls are ferocious and the best thing is that the rooms become free every ten minutes!

She laughs immoderately. LADY MOSLEY *looks penetratingly at her.*

LADY MOSLEY. Caroline, have you been drinking?

CAROLINE. Of course I have. Everyone drinks on aeroplanes. What's in your handbag?

LADY MOSLEY. I can't tell you. You might put it in your review.

CAROLINE. What review?

LADY MOSLEY. I thought you were going to review my book for the *Sunday Times*. Isn't that what you said on the telephone?

CAROLINE. No, I didn't say that at all.

LADY MOSLEY. My book is really rather rubbish, I'm afraid. I didn't want to write anything about the Duchess that only somebody close to her would know. It's so depressing when one's friends and family do that kind of thing. So I put everyone else's books around me in a semicircle, and I took a little bit here and a little bit there, but you're not to put that in your review either.

CAROLINE (*very clearly*). Diana, I'm not reviewing your book. I'm writing a profile of Maître Blum.

LADY MOSLEY. Whatever for?

CAROLINE. My editor thinks she's an intriguing character.

LADY MOSLEY. She's all of that.

CAROLINE. I think she's more than just intriguing. I think there's a wildly sensational piece about her just begging to be written.

LADY MOSLEY. You do?

CAROLINE. Oh, absolutely. There's something deeply murky and sinister going on here, I'm certain of that. What do you think of her?

LADY MOSLEY. Well, between ourselves, I find her rather frightening. She's so obsessive on the subject of the Duchess. She's loyal to her, of course, and that's quite admirable. But why has she locked her up? Why does she turn all Wallis's friends from the door?

CAROLINE. Is that why you had a bust-up?

LADY MOSLEY. Oh, I can't tell you the reason.

CAROLINE. Go on!

LADY MOSLEY. Well, you mustn't repeat this, but she'd taken away the Duchess's vodka.

CAROLINE *is shocked.*

CAROLINE. That's the most fiendish thing I've ever heard.

LADY MOSLEY. She said it was bad for Wallis's blood pressure. I suggested very mildly that one miniscule glass in the evening couldn't do much harm and she positively yelled at me.

CAROLINE. The woman's a nightmare. Worse than my mother, even. Would you believe, she actually told me if she didn't like what I wrote, she'd have me murdered!

LADY MOSLEY. She can't have meant it.

CAROLINE. Oh, she did. She screamed it in a *maniacal eldritch howl.* I'm taking it very seriously. Everyone knows French lawyers have mob connections. *And* she's a liar. Why did she say, one minute, that the Duchess was talking every day and then that Snowdon couldn't photograph her?

LADY MOSLEY. What?

CAROLINE. Oh, Diana, get a hearing aid!

LADY MOSLEY. I heard you. One can see, of course, why one dislocated royal would want to photograph another...

CAROLINE. But?

LADY MOSLEY. ... but it couldn't be done! It would be too grisly and gruesome to contemplate. The last time I saw Wallis, three years ago, she was slumped in bed like an old bag of larndry. Snowdon couldn't photograph her like that.

CAROLINE. He could prop her up.

LADY MOSLEY. No, propping her up would make her look much worse. Her big blue eyes were staring dementedly in front of her. I don't believe she even knew I was there. And something had gone wrong with her poor little hands.

CAROLINE. I thought her hands were enormous?

LADY MOSLEY. That's what I'm saying. They'd shrunk. They were like wizened little monkey's hands. She can only have got worse since then. There's a delightful man at the Embassy who said he saw her last year.

CAROLINE *reaches for her exercise book to make a note.*

CAROLINE. What's his name?

LADY MOSLEY. Oh God, I know him perfectly well and now I can't remember!

OFÉLIA *has come in. She hands* LADY MOSLEY *a glass of water and goes out.* LADY MOSLEY *finds a little box and takes out a pill.*

I have to take these for my stupid headaches. Lees. Walter Lees.

She takes the pill.

Blum let him peep through the bedroom door.

CAROLINE. What did he see?

LADY MOSLEY. I can't describe it. It's too awful.

(*Calls.*) Ofélia! I asked you to find Georges...

She turns to look for OFÉLIA.

Gorn, of course.

CAROLINE*'s interest is intense.*

CAROLINE. Diana, I've got to know this! What did this person tell you? *What?*

LADY MOSLEY. He said there was a ghastly pipe arrangement stuck up Wallis's nostril, and she'd shrivelled up like a prune.

CAROLINE. A *prune*?

LADY MOSLEY (*impatient*). You know what a prune is.

CAROLINE. Of course I do. My God, what a headline! 'Is the Duchess a prune?'

LADY MOSLEY. Yes, but Lees is a diplomat, and one can never trust people from the Foreign Office. So one doesn't *know* what kind of state she's in. Heaven knows what thoughts are going through her mind. I hope she doesn't *have* a mind. I hope her brain is a lump of grey porridge that doesn't work. Then at least she would have some peace. That old brute keeps having her operated on. One reads about it in *Le Monde*. She sends her to the American Hospital and they take some bits out and move the others around. What's the point? I think it's heartless to keep her alive. I wish she would die, I honestly do. It makes me blub like a baby just to think of her.

She is crying.

CAROLINE. And that beast took away her vodka.

LADY MOSLEY. I should never have told you that. Now please find Georges for me, and you'd better also make sure that old Blum isn't going to come bursting in.

CAROLINE. I will in a minute. Wouldn't you like one?

LADY MOSLEY. One what?

CAROLINE. A vod.

LADY MOSLEY. A *what*?

CAROLINE. A vodka!

She takes a half-bottle of Stoli out of her handbag.

LADY MOSLEY. Yes, all right.

CAROLINE *pours vodka into* LADY MOSLEY*'s glass, then finds a little ornamental cup and pours vodka into it for herself. She'll continue drinking until there's none left, but it doesn't make her slur her words or get woozy. In fact, her concentration becomes more acute in a hectic way. Meanwhile:*

CAROLINE. Blum says the Duchess didn't drink.

LADY MOSLEY. What nonsense. Wallis lived on vodka. That's why she kept falling over.

CAROLINE. Didn't the Duke notice?

LADY MOSLEY. Well, it was only after he died that she hit the bottle with such a thump. One's seen it before when a woman is left alone.

CAROLINE (*prickly*). One's seen *what* before?

LADY MOSLEY. Don't snap. Everyone knows that drink can be a struggle for a woman who's lost her husband.

CAROLINE. No, it's not. I've never heard anything so ridiculous as saying that people *struggle* with drink. If I *struggled* with something, I would *win*. What I am *doing* is what I've *chosen* to do, all right? Now, this is very important, because I need it for the *Sunday Times*. Was Blum really an old friend of the Duke and Duchess?

LADY MOSLEY. No, of course they were never *friends*!

CAROLINE. Did you meet her at their dinner parties?

LADY MOSLEY. Certainly not! Not even towards the end, when they were scraping the barrel for guests. She had some legal connection, I suppose, but I can't imagine it was very close. Wallis always boasted, you see, if she discovered a new manicurist or a masseur. She would have said, 'Oh, isn't it wonderful, I've found this clever old Jew who's going to look after the moneybags.' Blum is Jewish, is she not?

CAROLINE. I couldn't say. But what did they need her for? Didn't the Duke have one of the best legal minds of his generation?

LADY MOSLEY *laughs*.

LADY MOSLEY. You can't be serious! You could have worshipped the very ground he walked on, but you couldn't say he was intelligent in *that* way.

CAROLINE. What about the Duchess?

LADY MOSLEY. She was about as intelligent as our *proper* royals. Let's leave it at that.

MICHAEL *comes in from the smaller door.*

CAROLINE. Have they finished?

MICHAEL. No, they've booted me out.

(*To* LADY MOSLEY.) Good morning! Aren't you Lady Mosley?

CAROLINE. This is Michael...

MICHAEL. Bloch.

CAROLINE. ... Bloch. He's writing a book about the Duke and Duchess in the Bahamas.

LADY MOSLEY. Hasn't that been done?

MICHAEL. Well, yes it has, but...

CAROLINE. Michael, I want you to go back in and say to Georges that Lady Snowsley, *Mosley...*

LADY MOSLEY. ... *Mosley...*

CAROLINE. ... needs to speak to him at once.

MICHAEL. I can't. Lord Snowdon keeps glaring at me.

LADY MOSLEY. Give Georges a look. That's all he'll need. He's a very good butler.

MICHAEL. I'll do my best.

He goes out.

LADY MOSLEY (*of* MICHAEL). He's Jewish too, of course.

CAROLINE. I expect he is, but I wish you wouldn't bang on about it. It's thoroughly disgusting.

LADY MOSLEY. No, it's not! Neither Sir Oz nor I have anything against Jews *as individuals*. It's just that they behaved so dreadfully badly in the 1930s.

CAROLINE. Diana, if I wasn't trying to extort some vital information, I'd shatter this vodka bottle on your head. Now, what's all this about Georges? *What's in your handbag?*

LADY MOSLEY. I can't tell you. It might annoy old Blum, and then she'll slap an injunction on my boring book.

CAROLINE. What if I promise not to write about it?

LADY MOSLEY. Well, if you cross your heart…

CAROLINE. *Go on!*

LADY MOSLEY. Every time I've been to this house, I've noticed that something's vanished. A pair of Meissen dogs that used to be on this table. A portrait, there, of the Duke in his Order of the Garter robes. A Sévres snuffbox that used to be there. A Dresden mandarin here. And now…

She produces a small Cartier box from her handbag and opens it.

… do you know who I mean by the Countess Benevenista da Silva? She's a jolly old girl from Chicago and a very good friend to Wallis. She's visiting Paris, and she brought me this.

She reveals a brooch in the shape of a kingfisher, encrusted with jewels.

CAROLINE. Oh, that's extraordinary.

LADY MOSLEY. She bought it privately from Sotheby's in New York. Then a few weeks later, she was pasting some old photographs into her scrapbook and she found a picture of Wallis coming out of the Metropolitan Opera with the identical brooch on her lapel.

CAROLINE. How does she know that it's the same one?

LADY MOSLEY. Well, she doesn't. Only Georges will know for certain. But I must find out. She's dreadfully worried. She only paid seven thousand dollars for it and it's worth infinitely more.

CAROLINE. Was it a present from the Duke?

LADY MOSLEY. No, his presents to her always had an adorable little message inscribed and this hasn't got one.

CAROLINE. The whole thing's a message. It's a kingfisher.

LADY MOSLEY. 'King… fisher.' Caroline, you are clever! But then Wallis would never have sold it.

CAROLINE. Blum must have sold it.

LADY MOSLEY. I suppose she did. She does have power of attorney, after all…

CAROLINE (*explodes*). *What?*

LADY MOSLEY. I said…

CAROLINE. How did that *gorgon* get power of attorney?

LADY MOSLEY. Not so loud! Give me that.

She takes the bottle of vodka and puts it on a far table.

It was after the Duke had died, when Wallis was panicking over money. She was a little bit gaga too…

CAROLINE. My *God*!

LADY MOSLEY. … forgetting one's name and asking after people who'd been dead for ages…

CAROLINE. Jesus Christ!

LADY MOSLEY. … and always thinking the house had been broken in to. And when the police arrived, she'd say, 'Look, the burglars moved everything around and put it back exactly the way it was before, just so that I'd know they'd been here!'

CAROLINE. That was seriously gaga.

LADY MOSLEY. I'm afraid it was.

CAROLINE. So she'd have signed any bit of paper that was put in front of her?

LADY MOSLEY. I suppose she would. But if Blum's got power of attorney, she had a perfect right to sell the brooch.

CAROLINE *fetches back the vodka.*

CAROLINE. No, she *didn't*. Not for less than it's *worth*. If they'd *said* it belonged to the Duchess, it would have fetched a *fortune*!

LADY MOSLEY. Then why keep it a secret?

CAROLINE. Don't you *see*? That *ghoul* is keeping the money for herself!

TESSA comes in.

TESSA. That's it, we're finished. Tony's showing the old lady the try-out Polaroids. She's frightfully chuffed. He's going to chat her up about a certain other matter.

She indicates upwards.

You know, a portrait session with the Duchess. He thinks we're still in there with a chance. Let's hope he's right!

(*To* LADY MOSLEY.) I'm so sorry, we haven't met.

LADY MOSLEY. Lady Mosley.

TESSA. As in 'Sir Oswald'? Gosh! This has been quite a visit! Caroline, will you come and say goodbye to Tony?

CAROLINE. Tell him I'll see him in London.

TESSA. Will do!

She goes. CAROLINE *holds the kingfisher and looks at it.*

CAROLINE. Did the Duke adore her?

LADY MOSLEY. He was besotted with her.

CAROLINE. Did she love him?

LADY MOSLEY. I wouldn't have thought so. But she was utterly lost when he died.

CAROLINE. I know the feeling.

LADY MOSLEY. I'm beginning to know it too.

CAROLINE pours more vodka into LADY MOSLEY*'s glass.*

Oh, why not?

CAROLINE. The best time for me and Cal was when we were writing.

LADY MOSLEY. Cal?

CAROLINE. Lowell. I called him Cal. Everyone did. We were living in Kent. He was writing 'The Dolphin' and I was writing my first novel. But then every so often he'd make some mildly bizarre remark. I'd feel the same old prickle of dread and I'd say to myself that maybe it wasn't all *that* bizarre, that perhaps it didn't really mean anything. But then his mania would break out. Rages, delusions. Tearing down the wallpaper looking for hidden microphones. I can't describe how appalling it was to see the man I loved being so humiliated.

LADY MOSLEY *hasn't been listening.*

LADY MOSLEY. I've lost Sir Oz. I look at him now when he's dozing over a book, and all I can see is a leathery old Komodo lizard. There's not one trace of the man who could have been Prime Minister. And who *would* have been, if only the British had come to their senses. Britain would never have gone to war with Germany, if Sir Oz had been in charge. He had a very good understanding with the Third Reich.

CAROLINE *hasn't been listening either.*

CAROLINE. But I also resented it. I felt he'd abandoned me, that he'd turned his back on me and walked off into some tangled forest where I couldn't go after him. I hated myself for that. It seemed so cheap and vile to resent anything about a man who was so… so helpless. And I'd abandoned *him* when I handed him over to a bunch of doctors I didn't trust. So when he came home, things weren't the same as they'd been before. They couldn't be. There was too much damage. Between us, I mean. Much too much.

She cries.

LADY MOSLEY. Now it's as though some peculiar old stranger has taken over Sir Oz's body. It's easy to say, 'Oh, let him go, he's practically gone already.' But can one really feel that after forty-four years of marriage?

CAROLINE. Finally I moved to Ireland and Cal flew back to America. Back and forth, because neither of us could make up our minds. He arrived at JFK and… Do you really not know what happened?

LADY MOSLEY. Did you just ask me something?

CAROLINE. He took a cab to his ex-wife's house on West 67th Street, and it stopped outside. The driver thought he'd fallen asleep. But he wasn't asleep. He was dead. He'd had a heart attack. And on his lap was the painting of me that Lucian had done in Paris. Over the market in the Rue de Seine. *Girl in Bed*. He had his arms clasped tight around it.

Pause.

I've not felt right ever since it happened. Not writing much, because what's the point? Just stumbling from one grey pointlessness to the next. It's all shit. Isn't it all shit?

MICHAEL *comes in, catches the atmosphere and hesitates.*

What?

MICHAEL. Georges is on his way. He's taking Ofélia for a birthday lunch. I had to run to fetch him.

CAROLINE. Wait out there and warn us the instant the old tarantula comes out of the study.

MICHAEL. I can't do that!

CAROLINE. I thought you were on my side.

MICHAEL. I am.

CAROLINE. So what's your problem?

MICHAEL. I'm on her side too.

CAROLINE. No, that's no good. You've got to choose.

MICHAEL. I don't see why.

CAROLINE. Let me give you a lesson in life.

MICHAEL. I don't want a lesson in life.

CAROLINE. I know you don't, but this is a very important one. It is impossible to please two difficult women at the same time.

MICHAEL. But she's more difficult than you are.

CAROLINE. No, she is *not*! I'm *far* more difficult.

MICHAEL. You're probably right.

He goes. The big doors open and GEORGES *appears.*

GEORGES. Lady Mosley sent for me?

LADY MOSLEY. Yes, Georges, I did. Come in, if you please, and close the door.

GEORGES *comes in and closes the door.*

How long is it since you joined the Duke and Duchess's service?

GEORGES. Twenty-eight years, Your Ladyship.

LADY MOSLEY. You must remember some wonderful times in this house? The cocktail parties, the dinners, the footmen in scarlet livery?

GEORGES. They were incomparable times.

LADY MOSLEY. You love the Duchess, do you not?

GEORGES. I love her very much.

LADY MOSLEY. I believe I can say, as her very good friend, that she would rely on your discretion in this matter. Have you seen this brooch before?

GEORGES *looks at it.*

GEORGES. I could not say, Your Ladyship.

LADY MOSLEY. Look very carefully. You know all the Duchess's jewels. Is it hers?

GEORGES. I do not recollect it.

LADY MOSLEY. Thank you, Georges, that will be all. You're taking Ofélia to lunch, I believe?

GEORGES. She is waiting outside. Lady Mosley must forgive me that I do not recognise the brooch.

CAROLINE. Is there anyone else who might?

GEORGES. Perhaps the maid who dressed the Duchess on most days. But she has left the household.

CAROLINE. Who dressed her the rest of the time?

GEORGES. My wife, Ofélia.

CAROLINE *catches* LADY MOSLEY*'s eye.*

LADY MOSLEY. Would you call her in for a moment?

GEORGES *bows and goes out.*

Is there any more beastly task than interrogating the servants?

GEORGES *shows in* OFÉLIA, *who is wearing a magnificent full-length fur coat.*

LADY MOSLEY. *Ofélia, vous savez pourquoi je vous ai fait demander?*

OFÉLIA. *Oui, madame. Est-ce la broche?*

LADY MOSLEY. *En effet. Pouvez-vous la regarder avec attention, s'il vous plait? Vous pouvez la prendre.*

OFÉLIA *does.*

L'avez-vous dèja vue auparavant?

OFÉLIA. *Non, madame.*

LADY MOSLEY. *En êtes-vous certaine?*

OFÉLIA. *Tout à fait certaine, madame.*

LADY MOSLEY. *Merci, Ofélia. Oh, et bon anniversaire.*

GEORGES *and* OFÉLIA *go.*

So much for our suspicions.

CAROLINE. Oh, come on! Didn't you notice?

LADY MOSLEY. Notice what?

CAROLINE. When did you last see a coat like that being worn by a *mink*?

LADY MOSLEY. A *mink*?

CAROLINE. I mean a *maid*. What kind of *maid* wears a *mink* coat?

MICHAEL *comes in.*

LADY MOSLEY. But what does…?

CAROLINE. Don't you see? They're *all* at it. They're filling their pockets. They're stripping the house. They're robbing the…

She stops.

Jesus Christ. What if the Duchess is dead?

LADY MOSLEY. *Dead?*

CAROLINE. She could be, easily. She could have been dead for months. She could be in a frozen drawer in the American Hospital. Is there any evidence at all to suggest she's not?

MICHAEL. Ssh! She's on her way. I've just seen her.

CAROLINE. Oh, my God.

CAROLINE *rushes to a mirror, brushes the hair out of her eyes.*

LADY MOSLEY. Caroline, should you be doing this in the state you're in?

CAROLINE. I'm fine. I'm best like this.

LADY MOSLEY. Well, don't pick fights. Don't make silly jokes. Try not to ramble on forever and don't shriek!

MICHAEL *with his ear to the door:*

MICHAEL. She's coming.

They wait. The door opens and MAÎTRE BLUM *enters. She carries some Polaroids.*

MAÎTRE BLUM. These photographs are superb. Superb! I could tell at once that Lord Snowdon was *un véritable artiste.* Lady Caroline, you may examine them.

CAROLINE *takes them.*

Ah, Lady Mosley. Michael informed me that you were here. You have spoken with Georges.

LADY MOSLEY. I have.

MAÎTRE BLUM. I'm sure he has told you that the Duchess's regimen has been approved by Dr Thin. She has no need of the alcoholic stimulant that you proposed.

LADY MOSLEY (*stubbornly*). And the dogs?

MAÎTRE BLUM. The *dogs*?

LADY MOSLEY. The dear little pug-dogs that the Duchess was so fond of. Are they somewhere in the house? I haven't heard them.

MAÎTRE BLUM. Their yapping was too disturbing for the Duchess. They've been removed.

LADY MOSLEY. Removed to *where*?

MAÎTRE BLUM. I have found loving homes for them. You need not fear for their well-being. I like dogs much more than I like people. Michael, please accompany Lady Mosley to the door.

MICHAEL *moves forward to do so, but:*

LADY MOSLEY. Don't trouble yourself, young man. I know this house very well.

(*With intensity.*) Caroline, remember what I said.

She goes.

MAÎTRE BLUM (*to* CAROLINE). Well, my dear?

CAROLINE. How is the Duchess's health?

MAÎTRE BLUM. She is much better. When I saw her last night, she was sitting up in bed listening to Cole Porter music.

CAROLINE. But not dancing to it? What I mean is, do you think she could make a full recovery?

MAÎTRE BLUM. It would not surprise me. With a woman like her, there is no limit to what she can do. Which of those photographs of me do you think is best?

CAROLINE. This one here. Definitely. It quite reminds me somebody. Oh yes! Queen Mary.

MAÎTRE BLUM. Give it to me.

CAROLINE passes it back to MAÎTRE BLUM, *and she squints very closely at it.*

CAROLINE. What a shame it would be if the *Sunday Times* didn't print it.

MAÎTRE BLUM. Why would they not?

CAROLINE. They'll only print it if I write the profile. So you'll have to tell me a very great deal about yourself. You know what newspapers are like!

MAÎTRE BLUM. I *hate* to talk about myself. But I will sacrifice my privacy for my client's. *Je me sacrifierai pour la Duchesse!*

She goes to a cupboard, unlocks it and takes out an ancient and very large volume.

CAROLINE. What's that?

MAÎTRE BLUM. All of my life is in this volume. Cuttings from newspapers, photographs, letters. My soul is in here, you might say. I may consult it while we talk.

She sits.

I am waiting.

CAROLINE fumbles with the tape recorder. MICHAEL *helps her and it starts.*

CAROLINE. Well, I think what our readers would be most interested to know, is… how you first met the Duke and Duchess?

MAÎTRE BLUM. In 1924, my good friend the American Ambassador introduced me to them at a party. I was a lawyer at the Court of Appeal. My husband was also practising law in Paris.

CAROLINE. You mean the General?

MAÎTRE BLUM. *Not* the General! My *first* husband was Maître Paul Weill, who became the Duke of Windsor's lawyer.

CAROLINE. Was he…?

MAÎTRE BLUM. I'm trying to tell you. However, the Duke retained a lawyer in London…

CAROLINE. This was…

MAÎTRE BLUM. … a foolish old fellow by the name of Sir Godfrey Morley. He may have had a passable knowledge of English law, but of *French* law he knew nothing.

CAROLINE. How did *you* become their lawyer?

MAÎTRE BLUM. When the German Army invaded France, it was necessary for us, as Jews, to emigrate to America. I made a new career for myself. I studied and qualified in International Law! Shortly after we returned to France, my husband died, and I took over his duties.

CAROLINE. And then you married…

MAÎTRE BLUM. … General Spillmann.

MICHAEL. The General is a very distinguished soldier.

MAÎTRE BLUM. This is true and you must say so in your article. It is due to the General that France subdued the revolution in Morocco. The Moroccans all adored him.

CAROLINE (*annoyed at this diversion*). They didn't object to being subdued?

MAÎTRE BLUM. He was loved by those he conquered. I will give you an example. A young Moroccan shot at the General with his rifle, with the result that the General lost his…

She searches for the word. To MICHAEL, *who is offering to help:*

No, let me remember.

CAROLINE. His way? His temper?

MAÎTRE BLUM. He lost his shoulder.

Both MICHAEL *and* CAROLINE *look baffled.*

CAROLINE. Not his arm?

MAÎTRE BLUM. I did not say that he lost his arm. He lost his shoulder.

MICHAEL. '*Son épaule*'?

MAÎTRE BLUM *hesitates. Then:*

MAÎTRE BLUM (*with determination*). *Oui, son épaule.* Even after he lost his *shoulder*, his assassin grew to love him.

CAROLINE. But how could he lose his shoulder, without also losing his arm?

She starts to laugh.

How could anyone…?

She tries to stop laughing but without success. MAÎTRE BLUM *is icy.*

MAÎTRE BLUM. I assume that is all you need to know.

CAROLINE. No, no, I've got some very important questions still to ask. I'm sure the readers will want to know about the Duchess's business affairs.

MAÎTRE BLUM. Those are private.

CAROLINE. Not all of them, surely! Looking around me, I see so many beautiful… paintings, vases, statuettes… they must be worth a lot of money?

MAÎTRE BLUM. I don't know their value.

CAROLINE. And her jewels, her furs, her expensive luggage…?

MAÎTRE BLUM. What are you asking?

CAROLINE. Could you sell them if you wanted?

MAÎTRE BLUM. I act in accordance with my client's wishes. I mean her overriding wishes. She's not concerned with every *bibelot*.

CAROLINE. And who will inherit her possessions when she…?

MAÎTRE BLUM. When she *dies*? She will not die! Why does everyone want the Duchess to die? Every time she goes into

the American Hospital, the journalists ask me, 'When will
she die?' But there is nothing wrong with her! She will live
to be a hundred. Everyone in her family lived to be a
hundred!

CAROLINE. Has she made a will?

MAÎTRE BLUM. Every intelligent person makes a will.

CAROLINE. Who drew it up?

MAÎTRE BLUM. Who else but me?

CAROLINE. Why didn't Sir Godfrey Morley draw it up?

MAÎTRE BLUM. Because I had already paid him and sent him
away.

CAROLINE. *You'd sent him away?*

MAÎTRE BLUM. That English imbecile had drafted the Duke's
will so badly that, if I had not intervened, the Duchess would
have paid millions of francs in death duties and been thrown
out on to the street in her petticoat.

CAROLINE. Did you tell her this?

MAÎTRE BLUM. Of course!

CAROLINE. She must have been shattered.

MAÎTRE BLUM. She was.

CAROLINE. And so…

MAÎTRE BLUM. … she put me in charge of her affairs.

CAROLINE. And gave you power of attorney?

MAÎTRE BLUM. Naturally.

CAROLINE. It must have been a very distressing time for her.

MAÎTRE BLUM. It was.

CAROLINE. Was she a little distracted? A little dotty, perhaps?

MAÎTRE BLUM. Now I'm confused. Michael, what is she
saying?

CAROLINE *waves at* MICHAEL *to shut up.*

CAROLINE. Did she know what she was signing?

MAÎTRE BLUM. Of course she knew! She had an excellent business brain!

CAROLINE. Then why did she need to give you power of attorney? Either she was capable of running her own affairs, or she was not. Which was it?

MAÎTRE BLUM. She was alone in the world! As was the Duke, after he abdicated. He was *completely* alone. The French were very good to the Duchess. As for the English, why they didn't do the same, that's not my business. But she was surrounded by wolves and vultures! Must she have no one to sit beside her when Lord Mountbatten came for tea?

She mimics Mountbatten seeing a snuffbox on the table.

'Oh, Your Grace, what a charming little snuffbox! The Duke always wanted me to have it.'

She mimes his dextrously slipping it into his pocket.

Someone had to protect her!

CAROLINE. Why you?

MAÎTRE BLUM. Do you not know my reputation?

CAROLINE. I know it very well. That's why I'm asking.

MAÎTRE BLUM. *What?*

MICHAEL. My master has had some very illustrious clients.

CAROLINE. Such as who?

MAÎTRE BLUM. No more questions!

She rings the service bell.

Write your profile. You must make what you can of what I've told you.

CAROLINE. Who *were* these clients? What were some of your famous cases?

MAÎTRE BLUM. I will not talk about my cases!

MICHAEL. My master will not talk about her cases.

CAROLINE. I can't write an informative profile if she doesn't.

MAÎTRE BLUM. I don't want it to be informative!

GEORGES appears in the doorway.

Wait outside.

He disappears.

CAROLINE. Oh, this is absurd!

She goes for the book, but MAÎTRE BLUM *grabs it first.*

Give me that book.

MAÎTRE BLUM. No!

MICHAEL (*to* CAROLINE). You don't need to know all the details of my master's career. She's very well-known in England.

CAROLINE. No, she's not. It's just possible that she is in France…

MAÎTRE BLUM. 'Possible'? 'Possible'?

MICHAEL. There's *no doubt* that she's well-known in…

CAROLINE. Well, I'm writing this for English people and, I'm sorry, Maître Blum, but they haven't the faintest idea who you are. That's why I want you to tell me more about your life.

MAÎTRE BLUM. There is nothing to tell you!

MICHAEL (*quietly to* CAROLINE). Drop it.

CAROLINE. No, I'm not giving up on this. If Maître Blum won't tell me anything more, then I won't write the profile. And even if I did, they wouldn't print it.

Pause. MAÎTRE BLUM *stands clasping her book, staring at* CAROLINE, *her eyes blazing with fury.*

No more answers, no profile. Not even a photo. Most especially not a photo.

Silence for a moment. Then MAÎTRE BLUM *opens the book at random, darts across to* CAROLINE *and puts it on her lap.*

MAÎTRE BLUM. Look.

CAROLINE *looks.*

CAROLINE (*reading aloud*). Stravinsky. Charlie Chaplin. Rita Hayworth and Aly Khan.

MAÎTRE BLUM *speeds over to her, seizes the book, slams it closed and vanishes out of the smaller door.*

Why's she taken it away?

MICHAEL. French lawyers take an oath. They can't make use of their clients to seek publicity. If she showed you that book, she could be struck off.

CAROLINE. She could have shown it to me 'off the record'.

MICHAEL (*naive*). You mean it doesn't get printed?

CAROLINE *rolls her eyes.*

CAROLINE. Oh, for God's sake!

Pause.

When's she coming back?

MICHAEL. I don't think she *is* coming back.

CAROLINE. What?

MICHAEL. I think she's gone.

CAROLINE. Well, go and call her.

MICHAEL. No, I won't.

CAROLINE. Why not?

MICHAEL. She's had enough. All right?

CAROLINE. You mean she's gone for good? Oh *shit*, *shit*, *shit*!

MICHAEL. What did you expect? You were sarcastic. You got the giggles about the General. You went on and on about the will. You insulted her about her clients. Thank God you never got on to the other stuff. The Duchess isn't dead, I'm certain of that. And I don't believe anyone's robbing her either.

CAROLINE. Michael…

MICHAEL. Listen to me. *She doesn't want you to write about her.* She keeps *telling* you that because she *means* it.

CAROLINE. She agreed to talk.

MICHAEL. She *would* have talked. And then you messed it up. Think about that!

CAROLINE. So if she isn't robbing the Duchess, or keeping her corpse in a freezer, what's she doing?

MICHAEL. That's her business. Why can't you *leave* it at that? Why have you got to rootle around in the darkest corners of people's lives and put your *findings* in a silly, pretentious *colour supplement*? What *right* have you got? Is it engraved on a piece of marble somewhere, that behaviour that would be vulgar and cruel if anyone *else* did it, is perfectly fine if it's done by a *journalist*?

CAROLINE. I'm trying to get at the truth, that's all.

MICHAEL. *Your* truth. Not hers.

CAROLINE. Oh, ha ha ha.

MICHAEL. You were painted by Lucian Freud, all right?

CAROLINE. Well?

MICHAEL. Did his paintings look like you?

CAROLINE. They were his versions of me.

MICHAEL. Exactly. Versions.

CAROLINE. So?

MICHAEL. Robert Lowell wrote poems about you. What you said to him in the middle of the night, how you nagged him, how you fought.

He quotes from memory.

'If I have had hysterical drunken seizures,
it's from loving you too much.'

CAROLINE. I wrote that myself. In a letter to him.

MICHAEL. A letter to him. And then he put it in a poem and published it in a book. How did you feel about that? Didn't you find it very intrusive? Wasn't it hurtful?

CAROLINE. I don't expect you to understand this, but Robert Lowell and I were writers together. Each of us read what the other one wrote. So I knew what he'd done. I didn't necessarily like it, but I understood. A writer can't hold back for fear that somebody might get hurt. You've got to be ruthless. If you're not ruthless, then you're not a serious writer. You're an amateur.

She writes something on a piece of paper.

This is where I'm staying. Ring me if anything changes.

She goes. MICHAEL *looks at the address.* MAÎTRE BLUM *comes in through the smaller door, and goes to put her press-cuttings book back in the cupboard.* MICHAEL *picks up the Polaroid that* CAROLINE *admired, and looks at it.*

MICHAEL. It's really very like Queen Mary.

MAÎTRE BLUM *turns and looks at him. He turns, as though only that moment aware of her presence.*

MAÎTRE BLUM. Do you think so?

MICHAEL. Look.

He hands her the slide and she looks at it again.

There must be *something* more that you could tell her. Off the record.

She looks enquiringly at him.

That means it doesn't get printed.

MAÎTRE BLUM. You may make a small selection for her to read. But if one client is named in my profile, I will drag her by her hair through every court in France.

She gives him the book.

You are very good to me, Michael.

MICHAEL. I try to be.

MAÎTRE BLUM. I did not mean to say that the General lost his shoulder.

MICHAEL. What *did* you mean?

MAÎTRE BLUM. That he lost his *lobe d'oreille*.

MICHAEL. His ear lobe?

MAÎTRE BLUM. Yes, his ear lobe. I said 'shoulder' because I… In fact, I don't know why I said it. It came out while was searching for the word. You said *épaule*, and then I realised my mistake, but I did not want to admit it in front of her. I was afraid that she would think that my mind is failing. Do you think it is?

MICHAEL. No, not at all.

MAÎTRE BLUM. If I ever…

MICHAEL. What?

MAÎTRE BLUM. If ever it seems to you that my powers of thought are less… because of senile deterioration… you must tell me. Because I won't be aware of it myself. You must tell me in time for me to do what I need to do. Do you understand me? I refuse to be a breathing cabbage.

They glance momentarily at the ceiling. She goes to the escritoire, opens a small concealed drawer and takes out a small medical canister. MICHAEL stares at her, shocked.

This was given to me by a client, a doctor during the war. He said the effect is quick and painless. Now you know where it is hidden. You may need to remind me when the time has come. It's a disagreeable duty that I've given you. But I have nobody else to ask.

She holds up a hand to indicate, 'No further discussion.' Then she puts the poison back where it was and opens her book of press cuttings.

Let us examine this book.

She peers at it.

My old spectacles are too weak. I need a new prescription.

MICHAEL. Can you really not read it?

MAÎTRE BLUM. Haven't you noticed? Read to me what it says.

MICHAEL *looks at the book, still shocked and dazed. After a few moments:*

MICHAEL. It says that Sir Alexander Korda and Merle Oberon got married in your apartment.

MAÎTRE BLUM. There'd be no harm in telling her that.

She detaches the clipping and puts it to one side.

But 'off the record'.

End of Scene Two.

Scene Three

The salon. Several months later. Winter. CAROLINE, who has just been shown in, stares at GEORGES in great surprise.

CAROLINE. You said the *funeral*?

GEORGES. Yes, madame.

CAROLINE. When will it be?

GEORGES. On Saturday afternoon.

CAROLINE. There was nothing in the papers. When was it? Where did it happen?

GEORGES. At four o'clock this morning, in the American Hospital.

CAROLINE. My God, it'll be all over the news.

GEORGES *bows and is about to go.*

Georges?

GEORGES. Madame?

CAROLINE. Where will the funeral be held?

GEORGES. In Paris.

CAROLINE. *What?* Are you quite certain of that?

GEORGES. Quite certain, madame. It is the wishes of the family.

CAROLINE. The *family*? That's sensational. Is there a telephone I could use? I need to make a call to London.

GEORGES. Maître Blum insists that the telephone is left unoccupied. There will be many calls this morning.

CAROLINE. Yes, I'm sure.

GEORGES *goes.* CAROLINE *makes a note or two.*

MICHAEL *comes in.*

MICHAEL. Have you heard the news?

CAROLINE. Yes, Georges just told me.

MICHAEL. It had been expected for quite a while.

CAROLINE. Of course it had. I suppose old Blum will want to cancel my appointment.

MICHAEL. Oh, I don't know. She's bearing up remarkably well.

CAROLINE. She is?

MICHAEL. Oh, yes. She's asked me to write an obituary for *The Times*.

CAROLINE. The *London Times*? Is she expecting them to print it?

MICHAEL. I'm sure they will if she twists their arms.

CAROLINE. She'll have to twist them into spirals. They'll have vast pages of obituary on file.

MICHAEL. No, I don't think so. English newspapers don't normally pay much attention to French Generals.

CAROLINE. Who are you talking about?

MICHAEL. General Spillmann, of course.

CAROLINE. It's General Spillmann who's just died?

MICHAEL. Who did you think? Oh, not the Duchess! What gave you that idea?

CAROLINE. Georges mumbled something when he let me in.

MICHAEL. Did he mumble it in French?

CAROLINE. Don't try to be funny. I'm not in the mood. Not with widows piling up like dead bees in autumn. The Duchess. Me. Diana Mosley last month and now your master.

MICHAEL. Four widows.

CAROLINE. It sounds like a small Greek chorus.

MICHAEL. Or a very gloomy pop group. How could you think the Duchess had died, if you thought she was dead already?

CAROLINE. Did I?

MICHAEL. It's what you said.

CAROLINE. I said a lot of things that day. No, she's not dead. At least, she wasn't a week ago. I don't suppose you read celebrity magazines?

MICHAEL. No, but I've seen them on the bookstalls.

She gets a magazine out of her bag.

CAROLINE. This one's called *Ola!* I thought it would be rubbish, but in fact it's full of utterly riveting stories. It's a shame they're all in Spanish.

She flips through it with interest.

MICHAEL. Get to the point.

CAROLINE. Look at this.

She shows him a double-page spread of photographs.

MICHAEL. My God, it's her.

CAROLINE. She's gone *completely* black.

MICHAEL. How could they see into the garden?

CAROLINE. Upstairs window across the road.

MICHAEL. What are the nurses doing?

CAROLINE. One of them is lowering the Duchess onto the daybed, and the other one's holding out her arms to stop her falling.

MICHAEL. She looks like…

CAROLINE. What?

MICHAEL. … a marmoset. A very tiny one. Sort of paralysed, with its wiggly little hind legs dangling in the air.

CAROLINE. Look at her hands. Curled up like claws.

MICHAEL. And her face in the close-up.

CAROLINE. How would you describe it?

MICHAEL. Vacant.

CAROLINE. And?

MICHAEL. Desperate.

CAROLINE. And?

MICHAEL. I don't quite know where this thought comes from, but... Chinese? It's the way her hair's scrunched back in a bun.

CAROLINE. But what about prune-like?

MICHAEL. *Vaguely* prune-like.

CAROLINE. Only vaguely?

MICHAEL. Well, I wouldn't have thought of prunes if you hadn't mentioned them.

CAROLINE. Does she remind you of anyone?

MICHAEL. Nobody human.

CAROLINE. Take a good look.

He does.

MICHAEL. I give up.

CAROLINE. Maître Blum!

MICHAEL. No, you're imagining it.

CAROLINE. Oh, there's a very strong resemblance! The question is, did the Duchess get to look like Maître Blum, or was it the other way round? Like old ladies with their Pekineses?

MICHAEL. I just hope she hasn't seen it.

CAROLINE. She can't have done. She'd be suing them for the milk in their tea.

She takes back the magazine.

She sent a crazy telegram to the *Sunday Times*, threatening to sue unless I rewrote the profile.

MICHAEL. Yes, I know.

CAROLINE. Sue for what? There's nothing *in* the bloody profile. The paper's lawyers saw to that. It's just a pointless little filler. I don't know when I've been so angry. I've got a bloody good mind to write it all up again.

MICHAEL. For a different newspaper?

CAROLINE. No, I've had it with newspapers. If I could only be bothered, I'd write a Gothic fairytale. Set in a mouldering palace of mortality. Haunted by a necrophiliac lawyer issuing evil glances and murderous screams.

MICHAEL. Would I be in it?

CAROLINE. Why?

MICHAEL. Because I can't help wondering if you'd write about me along similar lines. I'm not a necrophiliac and I've never screamed at you, so you couldn't make fun of me in quite that way. But would you...

CAROLINE. What?

MICHAEL. Well, what would you say?

CAROLINE. I'd say what I saw.

MICHAEL. Such as?

CAROLINE. Your ridiculous jacket.

MICHAEL. Good job I ditched it. And?

CAROLINE. Your calling her 'my master'.

MICHAEL. I don't do that any more.

CAROLINE. Well done.

MICHAEL. Is there anything else that you might touch on in your characteristically acerbic tone?

CAROLINE. Only the obvious things.

MICHAEL. Which are?

CAROLINE. Your winsome smiles. Your jiggling from one foot to the other. Your ingratiating manner. Your desperation to please.

MICHAEL. Yes, well, one does get fairly keen to please, if one's trying to get somewhere in life. That's if you're not born rich and beautiful and there isn't a yacht race named after your family.

CAROLINE. Don't get upset.

MICHAEL. I *liked* you. Can't you *see* that? How would you feel if somebody you actually liked quite a lot wrote a book, and said things like that about you?

CAROLINE. But I'm not *going* to write that book.

MICHAEL. So there's no point my minding about it, is there? That's nice to know.

An awkward pause.

I'd better polish up my piece for *The Times*. I don't suppose I'll see you again before you leave. I'm sorry. I mean, for the way that this ended up. I did want it to work for you.

A small crash is heard outside the door: it's an ornament being knocked off a table. MICHAEL goes out and returns with MAÎTRE BLUM on his arm. Her eyesight is worse than when she was last seen.

Lady Caroline is waiting in here.

She shrugs away his arm.

MAÎTRE BLUM. Thank you, Michael.

He goes.

Good morning.

CAROLINE. Maître Blum.

MAÎTRE BLUM. I have still not received Lord Snowdon's photographs.

CAROLINE. I'll look into it as soon as…

MAÎTRE BLUM. Do so. I shall have little time to talk today. I have many arrangements to make. You know the reason.

CAROLINE. I'm dreadfully sorry…

MAÎTRE BLUM. But we are not here to speak about my bereavement. I await your ritual inquiry about the health of the Duchess.

CAROLINE. How is she?

MAÎTRE BLUM. She is better than ever. She talks and talks. She is covered in flowers.

CAROLINE. What kind of flowers?

MAÎTRE BLUM. Pink ones. Blue ones. What kind of ridiculous answer would you like to hear?

CAROLINE (*startled*). I was simply asking whether…

MAÎTRE BLUM (*savage*). Do you think it is clever to smile and raise your eyebrows to the sky and question every statement of mine that you do not believe?

CAROLINE. I'm not saying that…

MAÎTRE BLUM. It is my duty to put the best construction on the actions of my client. It's my *duty* and my *right*. So don't interrogate me. It's the accused whom one interrogates. I am *not* the accused. I will not *be* the accused. Do you understand?

CAROLINE (*shaken*). Shall we…?

MAÎTRE BLUM. … get down to business, yes, let us do that without delay.

She produces the draft of CAROLINE*'s profile.*

I have the profile of me that you have written. It appears that the *Sunday Times* was about to print it in this form, despite my many warnings about the need for me to approve it.

CAROLINE. I can't imagine what you…

MAÎTRE BLUM. Michael has marked my alterations in red ink.

She passes it to CAROLINE.

CAROLINE. We can do this another time if…

MAÎTRE BLUM. There is no question of a postponement.
Begin.

CAROLINE *finds a passage that has been marked. Reads:*

CAROLINE. 'Maître Blum is one of the oldest lawyers
practising at the French bar…'

MAÎTRE BLUM. *Supprimez ça!* Remove it.

CAROLINE. Why?

MAÎTRE BLUM. It is impertinent. Go on.

CAROLINE (*reads*). 'The Duchess lives in a prison-like house
in the Bois du Boulogne…'

MAÎTRE BLUM. You cannot seriously have thought that I
would accept that. It must read, 'The Duchess lives in a
house that looks like Buckingham Palace.'

CAROLINE. I could try losing 'prison-like'.

MAÎTRE BLUM. Don't try it. Lose it.

CAROLINE. 'The Duchess lives in a house in the Bois du
Boulogne.'

MAÎTRE BLUM. 'Like Buckingham Palace!'

CAROLINE. Oh, what the hell!

MAÎTRE BLUM. What are you saying?

CAROLINE. I think the best thing, Maître Blum, would be for
me to go back to London, read your corrections and put
every single one of them in.

MAÎTRE BLUM. Is this a trick?

CAROLINE *does her best to conceal her fury and distress.*

CAROLINE. No, it's not. But I don't work like this. I don't
write tosh. I don't write dreary little profiles. And I didn't
come here to write one. I came because I *thought* I could
write a piece of *genuine interest* about what's happening in
this house. Because I know for a *fact* that *something* is.

Of the profile in her hand:

As for this, I don't care what goes into it. Or what comes out. It doesn't matter.

MAÎTRE BLUM. Are you accusing me of something? Ask me a question.

CAROLINE. What for? You haven't given me a truthful answer since I got here.

MAÎTRE BLUM. But now I will. Ask me whatever you wish.

CAROLINE. Have you been stealing from the Duchess?

MAÎTRE BLUM *answers with equanimity.*

MAÎTRE BLUM. That was the question I expected. I charge a modest fee for my management of her affairs. I repeat: 'a modest fee'. In France, the more distinguished the client, the less she pays. That's our tradition. I could wish it were otherwise. The income from the Duchess's investments does not cover the cost of her medical care. That's why I am forced, from time to time, to sell some object of no sentimental value.

CAROLINE. What about the brooch you sold at Sotheby's?

MAÎTRE BLUM. A brooch in the shape of a colourful bird. *Un martin-pêcheur*, we call it. It cannot have been a present from the Duke, since there was no message from him inscribed on it.

CAROLINE. Why did you sell it in secret?

MAÎTRE BLUM. Isn't it obvious?

CAROLINE. Not to me.

MAÎTRE BLUM. I did not wish to humiliate the Duchess by letting it be known that she needed money. It is painful for me to admit that, even in private. I'm not an aristocrat like you. My father was a butcher. When I entered my profession, the prejudice against me was atrocious. 'A butcher's daughter'! And nobody wanted a woman to practise law. They said that a woman's voice was too high-pitched to dominate the courtroom. They said the jury and judge would laugh at her squeakings. They said that women, with their tiny brains, could not master the complications of the law. And that no one would want to be represented in court by a chimpanzee! All this I fought, and I succeeded. But I am still, *au fond*, a butcher's daughter. People like me do not talk about our money in front of strangers. We count it at night with the shutters closed. We bury it under the cherry tree where the neighbours or the tax-collector cannot find it. Because however much money we have, we smell starvation around the corner. The Duchess and I are the same in this respect. It is the basis of our *rapport*. She was born poor, and her greatest fear was that she would die poor. Thanks to me, she will not.

CAROLINE. Why was Ofélia wearing...?

MAÎTRE BLUM. ... Oh yes, the mink coat that caused you so much alarm. The servant borrowed her mistress's clothes for a special occasion. Do the servants not do that in Ireland?

CAROLINE. Why have you stopped the Duchess's friends from visiting her?

MAÎTRE BLUM. Most of these so-called friends are mere sensation-seekers.

CAROLINE. Why have you...?

MAÎTRE BLUM. The Duchess does not *want* to see them. Do you know better? Have you some insight into her mind? No you do not!

CAROLINE. Why are you keeping her prisoner?

MAÎTRE BLUM. If she's a prisoner, she is a prisoner of her age and sickness. Just as we all will be some day.

CAROLINE. Why are you keeping her alive?

MAÎTRE BLUM. She's keeping herself alive. She has a vigorous constitution. That is enough.

CAROLINE. One more question.

MAÎTRE BLUM. *Ask it!*

CAROLINE. Why did you take away her vodka?

MAÎTRE BLUM. It was making her ill.

CAROLINE. She was ill already.

MAÎTRE BLUM. It was not dignified.

CAROLINE. She didn't care about being dignified. Why did you do it?

MAÎTRE BLUM. Because I hated to see her drunk.

CAROLINE. You thought a single glass of vodka would make her drunk?

MAÎTRE BLUM. My dear, it's never a single glass. It's always the first of many.

CAROLINE. Why did...?

MAÎTRE BLUM. You of all people ought to know that! Look at you! Your eyes are blurred, your skin is aged. You were beautiful once. Now you are only beautiful on the walls of galleries. Well, if you want to destroy your life, that's your affair. But keep your anger about it to yourself.

CAROLINE. I'm not *remotely* angry. What are you talking about? It's rubbish!

MAÎTRE BLUM. You came to this house with one intention. It was to direct the hatred in your heart onto the Duchess. But then you found a better target. So you hated me instead. You pursued me. You manipulated me. You played on my vanity. You had criminal fantasies about me. You became obsessed with me. I don't understand it! What have I done to you? Who am I in your mind? Tell me! I am a lawyer. Nothing more. I care for a woman who was hated and reviled. A woman who the English hoped would die, in order to save their rotten Empire. I sit at her bedside every day. I stroke her hair. I see her smile. She...

She stops for a moment.

... she is so beautiful. Her skin is perfect. She has the lovely, soft body of a young girl. *Elle est belle comme tout.* And in her face, there isn't a single line of age. She has this youthfulness, this shining light. It is an inner beauty. It is the beauty of her soul shining through her face.

CAROLINE opens the copy of Ola! *and passes it to*
MAÎTRE BLUM.

What is this?

CAROLINE. Look.

MAÎTRE BLUM peers closely at it, then pushes it aside.
Cries. Wipes her eyes.

MAÎTRE BLUM. If you think that this is what makes me cry, I
must disillusion you. I have a better reason to cry today.

She gives CAROLINE *back the magazine.*

I know very well how the Duchess looks. I've been her
doorway to the world for seven years. In the days when she
could speak, she would complain to me that her hands were
cold. 'Hold my fingers,' she would say. 'Hold my freezing
fingers, just for a moment. Please, old Blum.'

She extends a hand.

I would hold them like this.

She holds CAROLINE*'s fingers. They stay like that for a few*
moments.

I would sit for hours. I didn't notice the time going by,
because I loved her. I loved her then, and I love her now.

CAROLINE. What do you think your love feels like to her?

MAÎTRE BLUM. What do you think it feels like?

CAROLINE. Like the most unbelievable cruelty.

MAÎTRE BLUM. No, my dear.

She withdraws her hand.

She is much wiser about love than you think. She wasn't as
beautiful as the Duke's other mistresses, and they were
younger than she was. There were a dozen princesses he
could have married. But he fell in love with a woman who
could never be Queen of England. So he lost his throne. It
made no sense. It was insane. But she accepted that insanity
as his sign of love. She knew that love, real love, reveals

itself not through miraculous, saintly acts, but through absurdities and mistakes. And yes, through cruelty too. This is the truth, or as much of the truth as I know myself. Let us lay it to rest in the space between us. Can I trust you to write no more about the Duchess?

CAROLINE. You edited the profile.

MAÎTRE BLUM. And?

CAROLINE. It will be printed with your corrections.

MAÎTRE BLUM. It seems that as well as losing my sight, I am also going deaf. What is your answer to my question? Can I trust you to write no more about the Duchess?

CAROLINE. I'm going to write a book.

MAÎTRE BLUM. What about?

CAROLINE. About her. Her friends. And Michael. And, of course, you.

MAÎTRE BLUM. Such a book would make me very unhappy.

CAROLINE *gets out her cigarettes and lights one.*

CAROLINE. I don't give a fuck how unhappy it makes you. Why should I? I don't respect you and I don't like you. I hate your snobbishness. I hate your bullying. I hate you for capturing the Duchess, and I hate what you're doing to her. Oh, and there's something else. I don't believe you. I think there are lies and gloatings and tortures that you'll never admit to. I'm going expose them all. There's just one thing that I'm grateful for. When I first came to this house, I didn't know what I was going to write next. Because I couldn't see the point. And now I do. It's a wonderful feeling. Thank you.

MAÎTRE BLUM. Well, you can waste your time if you want, but I will never allow your book to be published.

CAROLINE. You won't be able to stop it. I'll get the best lawyers to advise me. It won't be defamatory. It'll be public interest. Don't even *dare* to sue me.

MAÎTRE BLUM *smiles.*

MAÎTRE BLUM. My dear, I never sue. I merely *threaten* to sue. It's cheaper and it has the same effect. Publishers don't like to risk their money in litigation. Good day to you.

CAROLINE. Then I'll write it and I'll wait.

MAÎTRE BLUM. Wait for what? For me to change my mind? You'll have to wait until Judgement Day.

CAROLINE. I mean I'll wait until you die.

MAÎTRE BLUM *laughs.*

MAÎTRE BLUM. What makes you think I'll die before you? You drink. You smoke. I could live to be a hundred! All of my family lived to be a hundred!

CAROLINE. Then the book will be published after *both* of us are dead.

MAÎTRE BLUM. Then you will get no pleasure from it.

CAROLINE. I'll get plenty of pleasure if it's good. I care much more about that, than being alive.

MAÎTRE BLUM. Enough! Enough! You will not write about me!

CAROLINE. Oh yes, I will. And I'll do better than that. I'll make sure that I've *captured* you.

She goes. MAÎTRE BLUM *runs after her and calls through the door:*

MAÎTRE BLUM. I will live longer than you! Much longer! Wait and see!

She runs back into the room, rushes to the escritoire and scrabbles to find the secret drawer. She can't see clearly, so she pulls out a drawer and scatters the contents. Finds the secret drawer, takes out the canister of poison, wraps it in a handkerchief and crushes it under her foot. Staggers towards a chair and slumps onto it, panting and exhausted but with a sense of triumph: she has looked her death in the face and she has defied it.

You will be crying on your deathbed!

Captions:

MAÎTRE BLUM DIED FOURTEEN YEARS LATER AT THE
AGE OF NINETY-FIVE.
FOR THE LAST TWO YEARS OF HER LIFE SHE WAS
BEDRIDDEN, BLIND AND DEAF.
CAROLINE'S BOOK WAS FINALLY PUBLISHED ONE
YEAR AFTER THE DEATH OF MAÎTRE BLUM.
ITS TITLE IS THE LAST OF THE DUCHESS.
CAROLINE BLACKWOOD DIED ONE YEAR LATER.

Focus on MAÎTRE BLUM.

The End.

Author's Thanks

My thanks are due:

to Filip de Ceuster for help with translation.

to those friends of Caroline Blackwood who gave up their time to share their memories of her with me: Bob Crowley, Lord Gowrie, Jonathan Raban, John Richardson, Robert Silvers, the late Lady Spender, Hugo Vickers and Francis Wyndham, none of whom should be held responsible for any interpretations or misinterpretations of my own.

to Michael Bloch, who responded with great tolerance to being transformed into a character who perhaps only vaguely resembles him.

Finally, great thanks are due to Evgenia Citkowitz for guiding me through so many drafts with such a wise and generous eye.

Nicholas Wright